What's Awake?

Barn Owls

Patricia Whitehouse

www.raintreepublishers.co.uk
Visit our website to find out more information about Raintree books.

To order:

☎ Phone 0845 6044371

🖷 Fax +44 (0) 1865 312263

🖳 Email myorders@raintreepublishers.co.uk

Customers from outside the UK please telephone +44 1865 312262

Raintree is an imprint of Capstone Global Library, LLC a company incorporated in England and Wales having its registered office at 7 Pilgrim Street, London, EC4V 6LB – Registered company number: 6695582

Edited by Adrian Vigliano and Diyan Leake
Designed by Joanna Hinton-Malivoire
Picture research by Tracy Cummins
Originated by Chroma Graphics (Overseas) Pte Ltd
Printed in China

ISBN 978 1 4062 1236 5 (hardback)
14 13 12 11 10
10 9 8 7 6 5 4 3 2 1

ISBN 978 1 4062 1241 9 (paperback)
15 14
10 9 8 7

British Library Cataloguing in Publication Data
Whitehouse, Patricia, 1958-
  Barn owls. - 2nd ed. - (What's awake?)
  1. Barn owl - Juvenile literature 2. Nocturnal animals - Juvenile literature
  I. Title
  598.9'7

Acknowledgements
We would like to thank the following for permission to reproduce photographs: agefotostock p. 19 (© Gary Smith); Corbis p. 13 (© zefa/Helmut Heintges); Getty Images pp. 12, 17 (© Christopher Robbins), 21 (© Joe McDonald); istockphoto pp. 10 (© Inga Brennan - Photography & Design), 16 (© John Pitcher), 23f (© Andrew _Howe); National Geographic p. 6 (© Minden Pictures/Micahel Durham); Photolibrary pp. 9 (© Juniors Bildarchiv), 11 (© Dennis Green); Photo Researchers pp. 22, 23e (© Stephen Dalton); Photoshot pp. 14 (© Imagebroker.net), 15 (© NHPA); Shutterstock pp. 4 (© Dainis Derics), 5 (© Joanne Harris and Daniel Bubnich), 8 (© Daniel Hebert), 23a (© Yanik Chauvin), 23b (© Nick Biemans), 23c (© Newton Page), 23d (© Martin Wall); Visual Unlimited pp. 7 (Joe McDonald), 18a, 18b (© Robert Barber), 20 (S. Maslowski).

Cover photograph of a barn owl reproduced with permission of Corbis (© Mike Read). Back cover photograph of an owl's beak reproduced with permission of Getty Images (© Joe McDonald) and photograph of an owl's wing reproduced with permission of Shutterstock (© Nick Biemans).

 CAUTION: Remind children that it is not a good idea to handle wild animals. Children should wash their hands with soap and water after they touch any animal.

Contents

Some words are shown in bold, **like this**. You can find them in the picture glossary on page 23.

What's awake?

Some animals are awake when you go to sleep.

Animals that stay awake at night are **nocturnal**.

Barn owls are awake at night.

What are barn owls?

wings

feather

Barn owls are birds.

Birds have **feathers** and wings.

egg

Birds lay eggs.

Baby birds come out of the eggs.

What do barn owls look like?

Barn owls have white feathers on their faces.

Their other feathers are grey and brown.

beak

talons

Barn owls have short, sharp **beaks**.

They have sharp **talons**.

9

Where do barn owls live?

Barn owls live in dark places.

They build **nests** in caves, or in holes in trees.

They build nests in barns.

They build nests in piles of hay, too.

What do barn owls do at night?

Barn owls look for food at night.

They fly over fields.

Barn owls find something to eat.

They grab it with their **talons**.

What do barn owls eat?

Barn owls eat small animals that are **nocturnal**.

Barn owls eat mice.

Barn owls also eat **voles**.

A vole looks like a mouse with a short tail.

What do barn owls sound like?

Barn owls make a loud hissing noise.

They do not hoot like other owls.

A barn owl's call might wake you up at night.

How are barn owls special?

A barn owl can turn its head right round to see what is behind it.

It can hear very well, too.

A barn owl can hear better than it sees.

It uses its hearing to find food.

Where do barn owls go during the day?

In the morning, barn owls go back to their **nests**.

They sleep until it is dark again.

Owl map

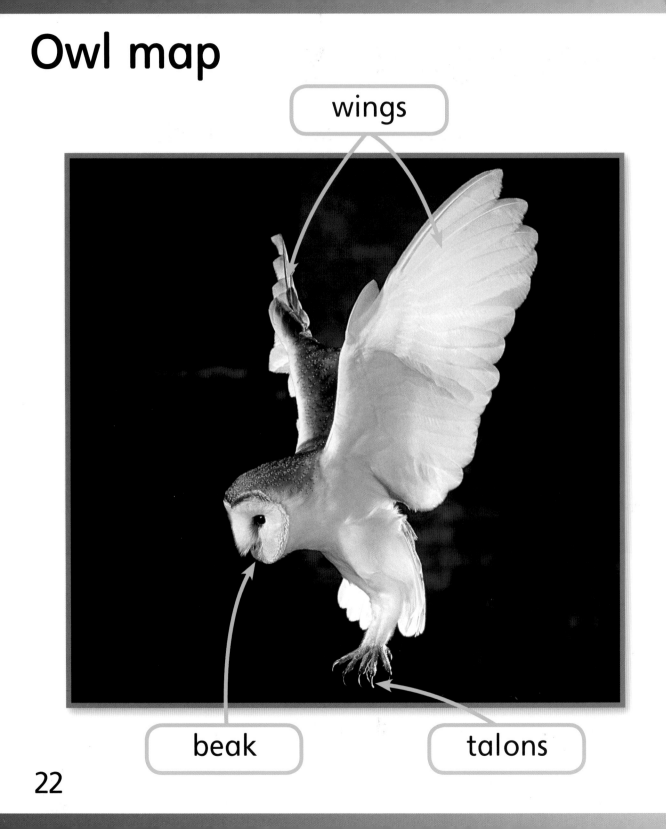

wings

beak

talons

Picture glossary

 **beak** sharp nose and mouth of a bird

 **feather** one of the long, light things that cover a bird's body

 **nest** place that birds make to rest and have their families

 **nocturnal** awake at night

 **talons** sharp curved toes on a bird's feet

 **vole** small animal, like a mouse with a short tail

Index

Note to parents and teachers

Reading for information is an important part of a child's literacy development. Learning begins with a question about something. Help the children think of themselves as investigators and researchers by encouraging their questions about the world around them. In this book, the animal is identified as a bird. A bird by definition is an animal that is covered with feathers and has wings. Point out the fact that there are many familiar birds in the world around us and help the children to identify them.